COOKING SKILLS

STEPHANIE TURNBULL

A+

Smart Apple Media

Published by Smart Apple Media, an imprint of Black Rabbit Books
P.O. Box 3263, Mankato, Minnesota 56002
www.blackrabbitbooks.com

Printed in the United States of America at Corporate Graphics, North Mankato,
Minnesota.

Library of Congress Cataloging-in-Publication Data
Turnbull, Stephanie.
 Cooking skills / Stephanie Turnbull.
    p. cm. — (Super skills)
 Summary: "Describes basic cooking skills and techniques, along with several
easy recipes from around the world. Includes glossary, tips and tricks, and
information on cooking careers— Provided by publisher."
 Includes bibliographical references and index.
 ISBN 978-1-59920-800-8 (lib. bdg. : alk. paper)
 1. Cooking—Juvenile literature. 2. Cookbooks. I. Title.
 TX652.5.T836 2012
 641.5—dc23
                              2011045977

Created by Appleseed Editions, Ltd.

Designed and illustrated by Guy Callaby
Edited by Mary-Jane Wilkins
Picture research by Su Alexander

Thanks to Isobel Walley

Picture credits
t = top, b = bottom
Page 2l Argunova/Shutterstock, r Perutskyi Petro/Shutterstock; 3 Fotosutra.
com/Shutterstock; 4t Jupiterimages/Thinkstock, b Iwona Grodzka/
Shutterstock; 5bl Richard Peterson/Shutterstock, all other images Thinkstock;
6l Carlos Yudica/Shutterstock, r Alistair Cotton/Shutterstock; 8, 9, 10 & 11
Thinkstock; 12 Jupiterimages/Thinkstock; 14 Thinkstock; 15 Sevenke/
Shutterstock; 16 Thinkstock; 17l Monkey Business Images/Shutterstock,
r George Doyle/Thinkstock; 18 Eising/Thinkstock; 19 Thinkstock; 20 Dick Luria/
Thinkstock; 21 White78/Shutterstock; 22, 24 & 25 Thinkstock;
26 Jupiterimages/Thinkstock; 28t Nick White/Thinkstock, c & b Thinkstock;
29 & 30 Thinkstock; 31 Shutterstock
Cover: Rido/Shutterstock

PO1444
PO 2-2012

9 8 7 6 5 4 3 2 1

CONTENTS

CLEVER COOKING

Do you want to cook fantastic food for yourself, your friends, and your family? Many dishes look difficult, but are really quite simple if you have a few cooking skills. This book gives you the know-how to make all kinds of quick and easy snacks, meals, and treats.

Getting Started

Before you start cooking, gather all your ingredients and equipment. Items like scales, measuring cups and spoons, cutting boards, sharp knives, a strainer, peeler, and grater are essential. Some recipes also use a blender or hand-held mixer. Unless a recipe states otherwise, each one serves four people.

▲ *Using the right utensils makes cooking much easier. Don't forget to wash up and put everything away afterwards.*

HINTS AND WARNINGS

Boxes with a lightbulb symbol contain handy hints for improving your skills.

Look out for exclamation marks too—these boxes give safety warnings and other helpful advice.

Using Your Head

Kitchens can be dangerous places. Here are some vital safety rules.

★ Be hygienic: tie back long hair, roll up sleeves, wear an apron, and wash your hands before and after handling food. Work on a clean surface.

★ Use a separate knife and cutting board for raw meat. In the fridge, keep raw meat on a covered plate on the bottom shelf, where it can't touch other foods.

★ Watch your fingers when cutting and slicing with sharp knives. Concentrate!

★ Handle blenders and other equipment cautiously. Never touch them with wet hands.

★ Remember that ovens and stoves get very hot. Use oven mitts, beware of rising steam as you lift pan lids, and turn handles inwards so you don't knock them off the stove.

★ Don't keep leftover food for more than two days.

★ Always get help from an adult if you need it!

Likes and Dislikes

When cooking for others, remember to check whether they are **vegetarian**, **vegan**, or have food **allergies**. Foods that can cause allergic reactions include milk, nuts, eggs, **soy**, wheat, and shellfish. Other people have an intolerance to certain foods, which means that they feel sick after eating them. Read food labels carefully to check what they contain.

ESSENTIAL SKILLS

Some basic cooking techniques come up again and again in recipes. Knowing them well saves you time, improves your cooking, and gives you confidence to try more complicated recipes. Here are a few vital cooking skills.

Peeling

To peel foods like carrots, first cut off the ends, then use a good, sharp peeler to slice off the peel in strips from top to bottom. Foods that don't need peeling must be washed well in a strainer.

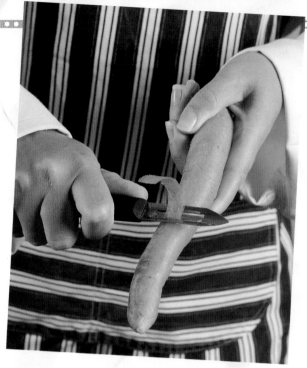

▲ *Peel away from your body so you don't risk injuring yourself with the peeler.*

Grating

Graters come in different shapes and sizes, but they all work the same way. Hold your grater firmly and slide the food up and down against the holes. It may help to rest the grater on a flat surface. Keep your fingers out of the way. If the food is too small to grate properly, chop it finely instead.

Chopping

When chopping a fruit or vegetable, cut it first so that it lies flat and doesn't slide around. Use a sharp knife, and don't try to chop too quickly. For foods with thick skins, like tomatoes, peppers, and egg plants, a **serrated** knife can grip the skin better. Chop into roughly bite-sized cubes, unless the recipe tells you differently. Bigger chunks may not cook through, and tiny pieces may turn to mush.

When grating lemon or orange zest (skin), stop when you reach the white layer. It's very bitter.

Greasing

Baking sheets, pans, and dishes need greasing to stop food from sticking to them while cooking. Just smear some margarine or butter on a paper towel, then rub it all over the inside.

Kneading

Kneading is a way of mixing dough to make it rise when it cooks.

1. Place the dough on a floured surface. Put some flour on your hands too.

2. Push a section of dough away from you with the heel of one or both hands.

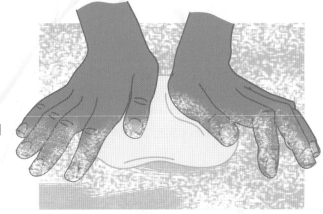

3. Now pull it back with your fingers and fold it over itself. Turn the dough and repeat for about ten minutes, until it feels smooth and stretchy.

4. Test the dough by pressing your finger into it. It should slowly spring back.

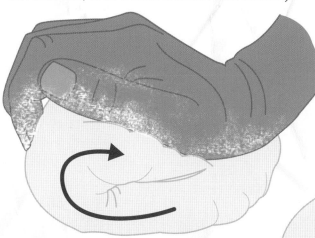

Be as rough as you like!

Mixing

There are many different ways of mixing! Whisking means mixing very fast, usually with a hand whisk or fork. Creaming means blending sugar and butter until they are smooth and fluffy. Folding means combining ingredients very gently, usually so you don't beat all the air out of them.

hand whisk

This book uses US measurements. Here's a handy metric conversion chart.

1 tsp = 5 mL
½ cup = 120 mL
1 Tbsp = 15 mL
1 cup = 250 mL

NO-COOK COOKING

Quick and easy snacks, lunches, and party food often don't involve cooking at all. Start with these simple recipes and test them out on your friends. As well as using fresh, healthy ingredients, you'll have plenty of chopping, grating, and mixing practice!

▲ *Crunchy vegetables make a good alternative to chips. Cut them into strips and serve with dip.*

Crunchy Coleslaw

You can buy ready-made coleslaw, but your own will taste much better.

You will need:
- ★ 2 carrots
- ★ ¼ white cabbage
- ★ ¼ red cabbage
- ★ few sprigs parsley
- ★ ½ cup yogurt
- ★ 2½ Tbsp mayonnaise
- ★ ½ tsp mustard
- ★ 1 lemon

1. Peel the carrots and grate them into a large bowl. Carefully cut the white cabbage into thin slices. Do the same with the red cabbage. Chop the parsley sprigs and add everything to the bowl.

2. In a small bowl, mix the yogurt, mayonnaise, mustard, and a squeeze of fresh lemon juice. Add the mixture to the big bowl and stir to coat the vegetables.

3. If you want, add extra ingredients, like apple slices, finely chopped red or green onion, raisins, sliced radishes, pecans, or walnut pieces. Pick and choose the things you like!

Don't make coleslaw more than a few hours ahead of time, otherwise the vegetables will lose their crunch.

You will need:

★ *7 oz. (200 g) smoked salmon*

★ *1 small tub cream cheese*

★ *1 lemon*

★ *chopped dill or parsley*

Speedy Salmon Pâté

Make this quick smoked salmon **pâté** to serve alongside the coleslaw.

1. Chop the smoked salmon and put in a bowl. Add the cream cheese and squeeze over the juice of half a lemon.

2. Whip everything together using a hand-held blender or food processor. Stop before the paste is completely smooth—leave some pieces of salmon to add texture.

Hand-held blenders are great because you don't have to transfer food to a different container.

3. Add a few grinds of black pepper, then spread your pâté on toasted French bread or small crackers, or serve it as a dip. Sprinkle a little chopped dill or parsley on top.

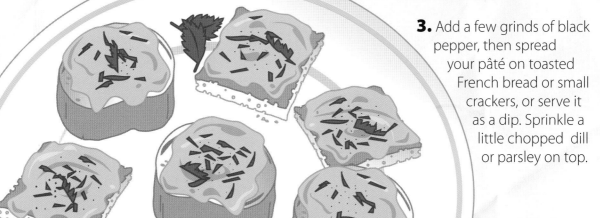

EASY MEALS

If you want to learn to cook, start with basic foods and everyday dishes. As you get more confident, add extra ingredients or try more complicated variations. Why not begin with baked potatoes or soup?

Super Spuds

It's very easy to bake a potato. First, wash and scrub a large baking potato. Poke the skin with a fork, then rub on a little sunflower oil—this will help the skin get crispy. Bake it at 400°F (200°C) for an hour. Push in a knife to check if it's soft inside. If it's not soft, bake it a bit longer.

Stuffed Potatoes

Next, try stuffing a baked potato. Slice off the top, scoop out the pulp, and mash it in a bowl with a pat of butter, a handful of grated cheese, and a spoonful of sour cream. Spoon the mixture back into the skin, then put it back in the oven for a few minutes to heat through.

◄ *Create all kinds of delicious stuffed potatoes by adding different fillings, like tuna, diced ham, or chopped green onions.*

Potatoes cook quickly in the microwave, but they won't have a crisp skin and don't taste as good. It's worth taking the time to bake them in the oven!

Soup Ideas

Soups are fun because you can decide which ingredients to put into them. Create chunky soups by chopping vegetables, frying them gently in a large pan with a little oil, adding beef, chicken, or vegetable **stock** and herbs and leaving them to **simmer** until the vegetables are soft.

► *Try including sweet potatoes and chickpeas in a chunky soup.*

Easy Peasy Pea Soup

If you want a smooth, puréed soup, try this simple recipe.

You will need:
- ★ 1 carrot
- ★ 1 celery stick
- ★ 1 onion
- ★ 1 Tbsp olive oil
- ★ 1 bouillon cube
- ★ 14 oz. (400 g) frozen peas
- ★ few mint leaves
- ★ 4½ cups water

1. Peel and slice the carrot, wash and slice the celery, and peel and chop the onion.

2. Put a large pot on medium heat and add the olive oil. Add the carrot, celery, and onion and mix with a wooden spoon. Cook them for about five minutes.

3. Crumble a chicken or vegetable bouillon cube into a measuring cup and pour in 4¼ cups of boiling water. Stir to dissolve the cube, then add the liquid to the pan.

4. Add the frozen peas, bring the soup to boil, and let it simmer for ten minutes. Take it off the heat.

5. Pick and wash the leaves from a small bunch of mint. Add them to the pan with a dash of salt and pepper.

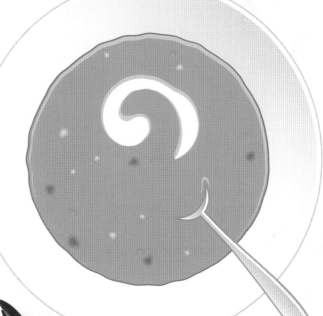

6. Purée the mixture with a hand-held mixer or blender until smooth. Heat it through, then serve. Try adding a handful of **croutons**, crumbled bacon, or a swirl of cream to each bowl.

SUPER ★ FACTS

★ The Spanish soup gazpacho, which is served cold, contains raw vegetables and stale bread.

★ Chinese bird's nest soup really does contain a nest—but not twigs! Swifts make nests from saliva, which hardens as it dries. In soup, it dissolves into a gloopy liquid.

★ Soups can also be made with fruit and served as a dessert.

PERFECT PASTA

Some chefs spend hours mixing, rolling, and cutting their own pasta, but don't worry—ready-made, dried pasta can taste just as good! It still takes practice to cook it just right. Follow these tips for perfect pasta dishes.

Cooking Method

You need to cook dried pasta in a large pot of boiling, salty water. Prepare 2.5 oz. (75 g) of pasta per person. Make sure the pasta is covered with water at all times, and stir it occasionally to keep it from sticking to the pot. Check the box for how long to cook—usually 10–12 minutes. If you boil pasta for too long, it gets soggy.

You will need:

Meatballs
* 6 saltines
* 1 lb. (450 g) lean ground beef or pork
* 1 tsp (5 mL) Dijon mustard
* 1 tsp (5 mL) dried oregano
* 1 egg

Sauce
* 1 onion
* 3 cloves garlic
* 2 tbsp (30 mL) olive oil
* 2 cans chopped tomatoes
* 1 Tbsp (15 mL) tomato purée
* 1 tsp (5 mL) oregano
* 5 basil leaves

Marinara Meatball Pasta

This fantastically filling meal has three parts: spaghetti, meatballs, and a famous Italian tomato sauce called marinara. Everything has to cook at once, so it will test your ability to multitask—a skill all great chefs need!

1. Meatballs first: put the crackers in a clean plastic bag and crush them with a rolling pin. Pour the crumbs into a bowl and break up any last big pieces with your hands.

2. Add the ground beef or pork, the mustard, dried oregano, egg, and a large pinch of salt and pepper.

3. With clean hands, scrunch and mix everything well. Divide the mixture into four equal-sized lumps.

▲ *Pasta can be served hot with sauce, or cold in a salad.*

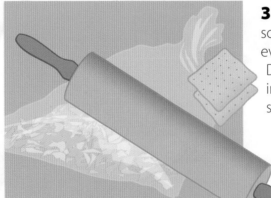

4. Divide one lump in half, then split each half into three. Shape each small piece into a meatball. Do the same with the other big lumps, so you end up with 24 meatballs. Cover the bowl with cling wrap and put it in the fridge.

5. For the sauce, chop the onion and finely slice the garlic. Add extra cloves if you really like garlic! Put everything in a large pan with the olive oil, and fry on medium heat for about five minutes.

Stir with a wooden spoon so they don't burn.

6. Add the chopped tomatoes, tomato purée, oregano, and a dash of salt and pepper. Wash and finely chop the basil leaves and add them to the pan.

Watch your fingers when chopping the basil.

7. Mix everything well and simmer gently, with the lid on, for about 25 minutes.

8. Heat a large pot of water to boiling, then add 2.5 oz. (75 g) of spaghetti per person.

9. At the same time, cook the meatballs in olive oil in a frying pan. Turn them with a spatula every few minutes. They will take about ten minutes to cook through. Check if they're done by cutting one open. If it's still pink, it's not ready.

Be careful when frying. Hot oil can splatter. Don't turn up the heat too high.

10. When everything is cooked, drain the spaghetti in a strainer and serve in bowls or on plates. Put the meatballs in the sauce, mix, and spoon on top of the spaghetti.

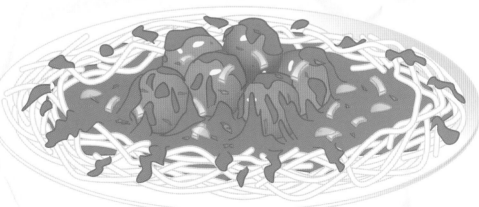

SPEEDY STIR FRY

Stir fry is the ultimate fast food—bite-sized pieces of meat and vegetables cooked at top speed over a high heat in a big pan called a wok. If you don't have a wok, you can use a large pan.

▲ *A wok has a rounded shape that makes it easier to mix and toss the stir fry as it cooks.*

You will need:

* ★ 1 lb. (450 g) dried egg noodles
* ★ 2 skinless chicken breasts
* ★ 1 onion
* ★ 2 cloves garlic
* ★ thumb-sized piece root ginger
* ★ handful snap peas
* ★ small can water chestnuts
* ★ 1 Tbsp sunflower oil
* ★ 2 handfuls beansprouts
* ★ 3 Tbsp soy sauce
* ★ 2 Tbsp sweet chilli sauce

Timing Tips

The key to stir frying is good timing. Prepare the ingredients beforehand, as they cook quickly in a wok, and you need to keep stirring. Add the ingredients that take longer to cook first. For example, don't throw in bean sprouts before chicken, or they'll be soggy by the time the meat is ready!

Chicken Chow Mein

Adding noodles to a stir fry creates a dish called chow mein. This recipe uses chicken, but you could try shrimp or **tofu** instead.

1. Boil a large pot of water. Add about 1 lb. (450 g) of dried egg noodles and cook them according to the box instructions— about four minutes. Drain in a strainer and set aside.

2. On a cutting board, cut the chicken breasts into thin, finger-length strips with a sharp knife.

3. Using a clean knife and cutting board, thinly slice the onion and garlic cloves, and peel and finely chop the root ginger. Wash the snap peas and halve them lengthways. Drain and halve the water chestnuts too.

4. Now you're ready to start stir frying. Heat a wok over medium heat, then add a swirl of oil and the chicken strips. Cook for about five minutes.

Stir with a spatula so the meat doesn't stick.

5. Add the onion, garlic, and ginger and stir fry for another two minutes.

6. Now add the water chestnuts, bean sprouts, and noodles. Mix in the soy sauce and the sweet chilli sauce.

Many supermarkets sell sweet chilli sauce—or try oyster sauce instead.

7. When everything is piping hot, serve in bowls and eat right away.

Stir fry looks best when it is colorful. Try mixing baby sweet corn with broccoli florets, carrot sticks, and red pepper strips.

SUPER ★ FACTS

★ Soy sauce is made from soy beans and salt, and has been used for more than 2,000 years in east and southeast Asian cooking.

★ Some enormous woks are designed for cooking on outdoor stoves. Chefs use giant paddles to mix a stir fry for hundreds of people at once!

★ Root ginger can be pickled, soaked in boiling water to make tea, or added to cookies and cakes. Some people also use it to treat upset stomachs.

BRILLIANT BURGERS

Burgers on buns are great for parties, barbecues, and any time you don't want to bother with knives and forks! Store-bought burgers can be full of fat and not very satisfying, so it's much better to make your own.

Hamburgers

For hamburgers, use the meatball recipe on page 12 and mold the mixture into six round, flat shapes, about ½ in. (2 cm) thick. Cook them in a frying pan for about four minutes each side. Serve them in buns with lettuce, sliced tomato, or grated cheese.

▲ *Slices of tomato and red onion look colorful and give your burger extra flavor.*

You will need:

* ★ 2 cans chickpeas
* ★ 1 red onion
* ★ 2 cloves garlic
* ★ parsley
* ★ 1 tsp (5 mL) ground coriander
* ★ 1 tsp (5 mL) ground cumin
* ★ ½ tsp (2.5 mL) chilli powder
* ★ I tsp (5 mL) lemon juice
* ★ 2 Tbsp (30 mL) flour
* ★ 1 Tbsp (15 mL) sunflower oil
* ★ arugala, cucumber, roasted red pepper strips
* ★ 4 burger buns

Falafel Burgers

Falafel is a Middle Eastern food made from chickpeas. It's a great alternative to meat and is high in **protein** and low in fat.

1. Drain the chickpeas and pat dry with a paper towel.

2. Roughly chop the red onion, garlic cloves, and a handful of parsley.

3. Put the chickpeas and chopped ingredients in a blender. Add the ground coriander, ground cumin, chilli powder, lemon juice, and flour. Don't forget a dash of salt and pepper.

4. Blend everything until it's well mixed but not completely smooth. Place the mixture onto a floury surface and divide it into four. Shape each lump into a burger.

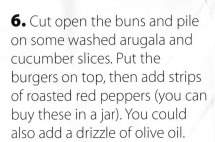

5. Heat the oil in a frying pan and fry the burgers for two or three minutes on each side. Flip them with a spatula.

6. Cut open the buns and pile on some washed arugala and cucumber slices. Put the burgers on top, then add strips of roasted red peppers (you can buy these in a jar). You could also add a drizzle of olive oil.

Warm the buns in the oven.

Tasty Tzatziki

You will need:

* ★ 1 cucumber
* ★ 1 tub Greek yogurt
* ★ 1 tsp (5 mL) mint leaves
* ★ lemon juice

Serve burgers with sauces or relish to put on top. You can buy tubs of spicy salsa dip and hummus, or make your own tzatziki, which is a Greek and Turkish yogurt dip. This goes especially well with falafel.

1. Cut the cucumber in half lengthways and scrape out the soft middle section (as this is too watery for the dip). Finely chop the rest.

2. Mix with the Greek yogurt. Stir in the washed and chopped mint leaves and a squeeze of fresh lemon juice.

Try this traditional way of serving falafel: shape the mixture into small balls, fry them, and serve in pita bread with a spoonful of hummus.

COOL CURRIES

A curry is any kind of spiced meat or vegetable dish. There are hundreds of curry types, some with creamy sauce or stew-like gravy, some fiery hot, some sweet and mild. A big pan of curry makes an easy, tasty meal, served with rice or warm **naan** bread.

Coconut Lamb with Sweet Potato

The secret to a great meat curry is to cook it gently for a long time, so the meat becomes really tender. This mild lamb curry with rice is a great recipe to start with. It works just as well with chicken.

▲ *Thick, creamy curries like this one are often made with coconut milk.*

You will need:

* ★ *1 onion*
* ★ *2 cloves garlic*
* ★ *thumb-sized piece root ginger*
* ★ *1.5 lb. (800 g) lamb*
* ★ *3 Tbsp sunflower oil*
* ★ *2 tsp mild curry powder*
* ★ *1 tsp ground coriander*
* ★ *½ tsp ground cumin*
* ★ *1 can coconut milk*
* ★ *1 Tbsp lime juice*
* ★ *2 sweet potatoes*

1. Chop the onion and garlic cloves. Peel and grate the root ginger. On a separate cutting board, cut the lamb into roughly 1 in. (2.5 cm) chunks (or use pre-diced lamb).

2. Heat the oil in a large pan and add the curry powder, ground coriander, and ground cumin. Cook the spices, stirring, for a minute.

3. Add the garlic, ginger, and onion and fry gently for about five minutes, stirring.

4. Stir in the lamb cubes, then pour in the coconut milk and lime juice. Add a dash of salt and black pepper, then bring the mixture gently to a boil. Simmer for about 20 minutes, stirring occasionally.

5. Peel two medium-sized sweet potatoes and chop them into roughly 1 in. (2.5 cm) cubes. Stir them into the curry and simmer for another 25 minutes.

6. While this is cooking, rinse the basmati rice in a strainer under cold water. Bring 20 fl. oz. (600 mL) water to a boil in a pot and add the rice. Stir and simmer with a lid on for 15 minutes.

7. Serve the curry with flaked coconut sprinkled over the top.

Not all curry powders contain the same ingredients, and some are hotter than others. Always check what it says on the jar!

SUPER ⭐ FACTS

★ Curries were originally from south Asia. The first curry recipe appeared in Britain in 1747.

★ Curry chefs often cook chicken and naan bread in a traditional clay oven called a tandoor.

★ Many curries use chilli peppers to make them taste hot. They range from very mild to extremely hot; the Naga Viper chilli is officially the hottest in the world.

Spiced Up Rice

Try turning rice a fantastic yellow color by adding a small spoonful of **turmeric** as it simmers. You could also heat a pat of butter in a frying pan and add a handful of almonds flakes and a handful of raisins. Fry them gently for a minute until the raisins swell up, then mix them into the cooked rice with a fork.

▲ You can also season rice by adding a few cloves or spicy seed pods called cardamoms.

BAKING BASICS

Baking means making bread, cakes, and other oven-cooked foods. It's a tricky skill to perfect, as you need to weigh and measure ingredients precisely, and get the cooking time just right. The key is to stick to simple recipes at first, and follow them carefully.

You will need:
- 2 cup (480 mL) bread flour
- 1 tsp (5 mL) salt
- 1 packet dried yeast
- 10 fl. oz. (300 mL) warm water
- 1 Tbsp (15 mL) olive oil

Don't use hot water, or the yeast won't work.

Pizza Crust
A fun way to start baking is to make bread dough for pizza crusts.

1. Sift the flour into a large mixing bowl. Add the salt and dried yeast. Make a hollow in the middle and pour in the warm water and olive oil.

2. Mix into a smooth dough with a wooden spoon. Add a few drops of water if it's dry, or a sprinkling of flour if it's sticky.

3. Now put the dough on a floured board and knead for about ten minutes (see page 7), until it feels smooth and stretchy.

4. Put the dough back in the bowl and cover with a dish towel. Set it in a warm place for about an hour and a half. The yeast will m the dough double in size during this time.

5. While the dough rises, make the marinara sauce from page 13—but just use one can of tomatoes. Simmer for about half an hour, so it's nice and thick, then leave it to cool.

6. Divide the dough into four pieces and roll out each one on a floured surface. Make them circular and about ½ in. (1 cm) thick. Lay them on greased baking sheets. Heat the oven to 425°F (220°C).

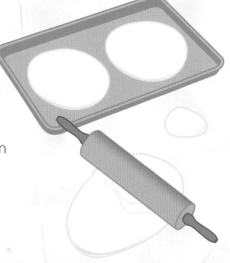

7. Smooth a large tablespoon of the sauce over each crust, then cover with thin slices of mozzarella cheese. Add a mixture of toppings (be creative!) and finish with grated cheddar cheese.

You could try:

A pepperoni, onions, and green pepper

B smoked ham and pineapple

C mushrooms, olives, and tomato

8. Cook the pizzas for about 12 minutes until the edges are golden and the cheese is melted. Be careful not to overcook and burn them.

▲ *Italian mozzarella cheese is ideal for pizzas because it gets gooey and stretchy when cooked.*

For a party, make the crusts and sauce beforehand and store in the fridge. When friends arrive, spread the sauce and put out bowls of different toppings, so everyone can create their own pizza.

Breadsticks

To make breadsticks, follow steps 1 to 4, then knead the dough for a few minutes and divide it into eight sticks. Put the sticks on a greased baking sheet and leave to rise again for 20 minutes. Brush with milk and sprinkle with flour, then bake in a preheated oven at 400°F (200°C) for 10–15 minutes, until the breadsticks are golden brown on top.

DELICIOUS DESSERTS

Every good cook needs a few really great dessert recipes up their sleeve, so here are two unique dishes to try. Remember that they're very sweet and filling, so they're best saved for special occasions when you really want to wow your friends and family.

You will need:

★ 1 packet graham crackers

★ 5 Tbsp. butter

★ 16 oz. (475 g) cream cheese

★ ¾ cup powdered sugar

★ 1 lime

★ 1 tsp (5 mL) vanilla extract

★ 7 fl. oz. (200 mL) heavy cream

Lime Cheesecake

This cheesecake tastes great—and, best of all, it doesn't involve any cooking. It's worth buying a springform cake pan with a separate base, otherwise you'll have trouble removing your finished cheesecake.

1. In a bowl, crush crackers into fine crumbs with the end of a rolling pin or your fingers.

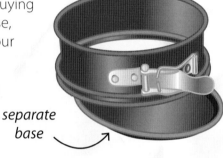

separate base

5. Ease the cheesecake out of the pan and top with sliced fruit or a fruit compote (see page 24). It will serve about eight people.

2. Melt the butter, add to the crumbs, and stir. Grease the pan, spoon in the cracker crust and press flat. Put it in the fridge for an hour.

3. Put the cream cheese in a large bowl. Add the powdered sugar and cream it with a wooden spoon. Grate in the zest of a lime, then squeeze in the juice. Stir in the vanilla extract.

4. In another bowl, whip the heavy cream until it thickens. Gently stir it into the mixture, a few spoonfuls at a time. Empty the mixture into the cake pan, spread it evenly, and refrigerate for at least an hour.

Speedy Treacle Pudding

Try this traditional British dessert. It takes only seven minutes to cook!

You will need:
★ ½ cup (120 mL) butter
★ ½ cup (120 mL) superfine sugar
★ 2 eggs
★ 2 Tbsp (30 mL) milk
★ ¾ cup (180 mL) flour
★ 1 orange
★ ½ c. (120 mL) corn syrup

1. Cream the butter and sugar in a mixing bowl.

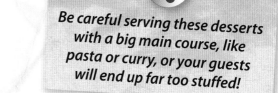

Be careful serving these desserts with a big main course, like pasta or curry, or your guests will end up far too stuffed!

2. In a separate bowl, beat the eggs and milk, then stir into the butter and sugar mixture.

3. Sift in the flour and mix. Add the grated zest of an orange, then squeeze in the juice of half the orange.

4. Draw around the top of a large microwave dish on wax paper. Cut out the circle.

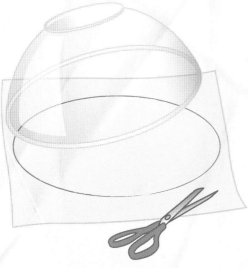

5. Grease the dish, and spoon in the corn syrup. Pour the pudding mixture on top. Grease the circle of paper and put it on top, butter side down.

6. Bake in a microwave for seven minutes on medium power, then let stand for a few minutes. Remove the wax paper, put a plate on top of the dish and turn everything upside down so the pudding falls on to the plate. Serve with custard sauce.

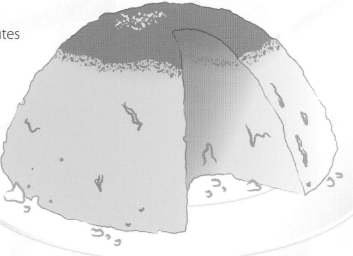

FRUIT FEASTS

Fruit is perfect if you want to finish your meal with a lighter dessert. Try making a fruit salad with your favorite fruits—and experiment with a few you've never tried before. How about lychees, mangoes, dragon fruit, or ugli fruit? See what you can find in stores!

You will need:

- ★ 2 cups mixed berries
- ★ 2 Tbsp superfine sugar
- ★ 3 Tbsp water
- ★ granola
- ★ ice cream

Berry Compotes

A compote is a sweet fruit purée. Compotes are often made with berries like raspberries, blackberries, strawberries, and blueberries.

Create smoothies by mixing chopped fruit in a blender. Add milk or plain yogurt for a creamier drink, or a spoonful of honey as a sweetener.

1. Rinse the berries in a strainer and heat them gently in a large pot with the sugar and water.

2. Once the mixture is simmering, remove from the heat and strain to remove seeds and other pieces.

3. In a tall glass, create layers of compote, ice cream, and crunchy granola. This kind of dessert is called a parfait.

Use Greek yogurt instead of ice cream for a breakfast dish.

Baked Spiced Apples

One of the tastiest hot fruit desserts is a baked apple. Use cooking apples, or any large, slightly tart eating apples.

You will need:

* ★ 4 apples
* ★ 4 Tbsp (60 mL) dark brown sugar
* ★ 1 tsp (5 mL) all-spice
* ★ handful raisins
* ★ handful chopped pecans or walnuts
* ★ 4 tsp (5 mL) butter or margarine

1. Preheat the oven to 400°F (200°C). Wash four large apples and remove the cores. Place the apples in a shallow baking dish.

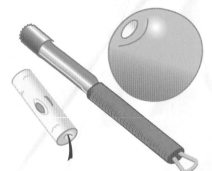

Use an apple corer.

2. In a small bowl, mix the brown sugar, all-spice, raisins, and chopped nuts.

3. Fill the apples with the mixture and sprinkle any extra around the apples. Put a teaspoon of butter or margarine on top of each apple and pour a little water into the dish.

4. Put on a low rack in the oven and bake for 15 minutes, then remove and spoon some of the syrupy liquid on top of the apples to keep them moist. Put back in the oven for another 10–15 minutes. Serve with the juice poured on top.

★ There are more than 7,500 kinds of apples worldwide.

★ Pineapples are a type of berry. They got their name because they look like pine cones.

SUPER ★ FACTS

★ Some wild bananas are pink, red, or have green and white stripes. Some are very fat and others are shorter than your little finger!

SWEET SNACKS

Treats like cakes and cookies are fun to make and ideal for parties and picnics—or even to wrap in a gift box and give as a present. Here are a couple of useful recipes to start you off.

You will need:
- ★ ½ cup butter
- ★ ¼ cup sugar
- ★ 1 cup plain flour
- ★ ⅓ cup chocolate chips

Chocolate Chip Cookies

Here's an easy chocolate chip cookie recipe. To make shortbread cookies instead, just leave out the chips.

1. Heat the oven to 325°F (170°C) In a bowl, cream the butter and sugar.

2. Stir in the flour and mix to a smooth dough, then stir in the chocolate chips.

3. Shape the dough into a fat sausage, wrap it in cling wrap and chill in the fridge for 20 minutes.

4. Cut the dough into thick rounds and arrange on a greased baking sheet. Bake for 10–15 minutes until they're a pale golden color. Carefully move them onto a wire rack to cool.

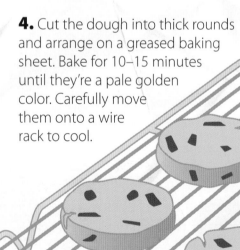

You can also, roll out the dough and cut shapes with cookie cutters.

Fruity Bran Muffins

These fantastic muffins are low in fat, full of fruit, and use bananas instead of lots of sugar. Just remember to make the muffin mixture well in advance, so that the bran and fruit have plenty of time to soften and swell up.

You will need:

- ★ 2 c. (480 mL) bran cereal
- ★ ½ c. (120 mL) dried apricots
- ★ ½ c. (120 mL) dried cranberries
- ★ 1 c. (250 mL) brown sugar
- ★ 1½ Tbsp (22 mL) corn syrup
- ★ 1½ c. (310 mL) milk
- ★ 1 c. (250 mL) flour
- ★ 2 bananas

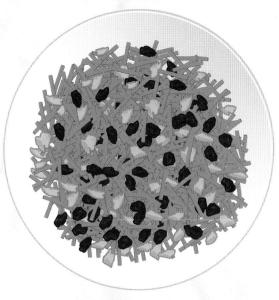

Try different dried fruit, like figs or dates, and add chopped nuts too.

1. Put the bran cereal, dried apricots, and cranberries into a large bowl.

2. Add the sugar and corn syrup. Pour the milk over and mix well. Cover the bowl and refrigerate for a few hours or overnight.

3. Heat the oven to 325°F (170°C). Mash the bananas and stir them into the mixture, along with the flour.

4. Spoon into a greased muffin tin and bake for about 15 minutes, until the muffins have risen and are golden brown. Remove them carefully and let cool on a wire rack.

The mixture makes about 24 muffins, so you may need to cook them in several batches. Save some by freezing a batch once they've cooled.

Temperatures and times for baking vary hugely with different ovens. Experiment to find out how long cookies and cakes take to brown in your oven.

WHAT NEXT?

The key to improving and expanding your cooking skills is to keep cooking! Search for recipes online and in the library, or ask relatives for their tried and tested favorites. Don't be afraid to experiment with ingredients or make up your own variations on recipes—after all, that's how celebrity chefs got started!

World Food

Be open-minded when it comes to trying recipes. Look at dishes from other countries—how about Caribbean **jerk chicken**, Thai curry, Japanese **sushi** (below), Spanish **paella**, or Moroccan **tagine**? If you go abroad, make a note of tasty ingredients and look for them at home.

Home Growing

Herbs such as basil, thyme, and mint are easy to grow in pots on your windowsill or outside. If you have space, try making a small vegetable garden. Cooking with ingredients you've grown yourself is very satisfying and saves money too.

▲ *Restaurant chefs plan dishes carefully, using a wide range of ingredients.*

Taking it Further

It helps to learn from an expert, so find out whether there are any cooking classes or workshops in your area. If you're serious about cooking as a career, look up college and university courses. Cook for friends and ask for their honest opinion—but be prepared to take criticism!

▲ *These clever rose sculptures are carved out of a melon and carrot pieces.*

Careers in Food

If you have the skills and stamina to work in a hot, busy kitchen, you could become a chef, and even end up running your own restaurant. Or how about training as a butcher, baker, or cake decorator? Perhaps you could be a nutritionist, advising people on healthy foods, or even an artist who makes food sculptures!

▼ *Cake decorators use special icing to cover cakes and create delicate and complicated features like flowers.*

GLOSSARY

allergies
An extreme sensitivity to something, which usually leads to reactions like sneezing and skin rashes, or sometimes even dizziness and difficulty breathing.

crouton
A small crunchy cube of baked or fried bread. You can try making your own croutons, or buy them pre-made.

garnish
A small piece of food used to decorate and add extra flavor to a dish.

jerk chicken
A dish of chicken coated in hot spices and grilled or barbecued to give it a strong smoky flavor.

naan
A flat bread from south and central Asia. Some types of naan have fillings like raisins, nuts, onions, or ground meat.

paella
A dish made by simmering rice, stock, herbs, and vegetables, plus seafood or meat.

pâté
A paste of finely ground meat.

protein
A substance found in animals and plants that is vital for building cells in your body and keeping bones, muscles, skin, and other body parts strong and healthy.

serrated
A blade with notches, or teeth, like a saw.

simmer
To keep a liquid cooking gently at just under boiling. First heat the liquid until it boils, then turn down the heat until there are hardly any bubbles.

soy
An East Asian plant that produces edible beans, used to make foods such as soy milk, tofu, and soy sauce.

stock
Water flavored with meat, vegetables, herbs, or spices. Some cooks simmer their own stock, but the easiest method is to dissolve dried bouillon cubes in hot water.

sushi
Cooked rice combined with ingredients like seafood, vegetables, and seaweed.

tagine
A slow-cooked stew made in a big clay pot with a lid.

tofu
A food made from soy beans and water, pressed into blocks that look like white cheese; tofu can be used in savory and sweet dishes.

turmeric
A south Asian plant that is dried and ground into a peppery, orange powder.

vegan
Someone who doesn't eat any food that comes from animals, including meat, eggs, and dairy products.

vegetarian
Someone who doesn't eat meat. Some vegetarians avoid other animal products too.

USEFUL WEBSITES

www.activitytv.com/cooking-with-kids
Browse through lots of fun and easy recipes and watch helpful videos showing you how to make each one.

www.spatulatta.com
Find all kinds of kid-friendly recipes, learn some new cooking skills, and watch videos of cooking techniques at this website.

www.marthastewart.com/cooking-with-kids
Entertainment maven Martha Stewart shares ideas for making superfun main dishes, desserts, and party foods.

www.kidsacookin.org
Kids a Cookin' is where cooking is fun! Follow Karen Arnold as she teaches kids how to make delicious and nutritious food.

www.careerplanning.about.com/library/quiz/career_quizzes/blchef_quiz.htm
Answer a quiz to discover whether you have the right skills to become a chef, then find out more about career options in cooking.

INDEX